D1342901

Ritual Lights

Joelle Barron

RITUAL LIGHTS

icehouse poetry
an imprint of Goose Lane Editions

Edited by Leah Horlick.
Cover and page design by Julie Scriver.
Cover image by Robson Hatsukami Morgan, Unsplash.com.
Printed in Canada.
10 9 8 7 6 5 4 3 2 1

Library and Archives Canada Cataloguing in Publication

Barron, Joelle, 1990-, author
    Ritual lights / Joelle Barron.

Poems.
Issued in print and electronic formats.
ISBN 978-1-77310-018-0 (softcover).--ISBN 978-1-77310-019-7 (EPUB).--
ISBN 978-1-77310-020-3 (Kindle)

    I. Title.

PS8603.A7713R58 2018   C811'.6   C2017-905586-0
                                           C2017-905587-9

We acknowledge the generous support of the Government of Canada, the Canada Council for the Arts, and the Government of New Brunswick.

Goose Lane Editions
500 Beaverbrook Court, Suite 330
Fredericton, New Brunswick
CANADA E3B 5X4
www.gooselane.com

for Katy

What is love?
My questions were not original.
Nor did I answer them.
　　— Anne Carson, "The Glass Essay"

Contents

I'm a Scholar of Nothing

I read somewhere, in Persephone's
most ancient myth, she heard caws
of the lonesome dead vibrato up
the grass between her rough toes,
and she went to them.

In the beginning, there was no Hades.
He appeared, a real George Costanza,
and gorged hell's pomegranate
so he could crash.

I'm telling you the myth
I've decided on. I guess
that's the Demeter in me.

Listen: rape yarns are seldom
what they should be. If you knew
the ancient work of thrashing girls,
by brain and body, into pale submission,
I could be a scholar of that.

So Many People Write Poems about Her

The way I tell it, Hades
is the last man of many
Persephone fucks
before she realizes
she's a lesbian.

Once, an entire population
of alpha-male baboons
was wiped out from eating
bad garbage. Only took
one generation of monkeys
raised gently by women
to change the culture
of monkeys forever.

My myth does away
with rapist gods, Olympian
alpha monkeys. All men.
Maybe it was bad ambrosia.
Nothing left but sisters,
self-replicating on clouds.

Little Girl/Chaos Bringer

> You must ask yourself:
> where is it snowing?
>
> — Louise Glück, "Persephone the Wanderer"

Louise's poem, the mother
chops her daughter
into chuck. In mythology,
as in popular culture,
mothers are often worse

than rapists. Sometimes I feel
like a bad mother because I don't pretend
to possess you. Honestly,

you frighten me. Demeter named her daughter
Kore, *little girl*. Mothers get pissed
when their children get tattoos, or change
names for non-marriage reasons. I guess
I'd be pissed if you voted
Conservative. I gave you

a little girl name, but already
you're more of a Persephone, *chaos bringer*,
kind of reckless I've longed
to be since high school English

class. Your mom's interpretation:
Persephone was plucked
by her husband, made the best of her winters
in hell, like an Arizona snowbird. Whipped
that place into shape. I'm afraid

of you because you made me see
how weak I am. Little line squall
in my living room. Rising up each
morning, spring flowers spilling
from under your feet.

My Hades

Hades No. 1: around the same time
as Disney's 1997 James Woods
blue flame haircut. Used to play
domination with Barbies, learned
the painful/good/terrible ache
of being held down.

Hades No. 2: basement suite,
housemate with a Volcano vape
who'd come home from work
drunk, careen into my room.
I didn't fight him; instead,
snuck my terror-rotted
guts to Starbucks at 5 AM,
got diarrhea in the bathroom.
Spared him
my body's grossness.

Hades No. 3: walked into hell
with him. A medieval-themed
tavern, pretending I liked men,
their lagers. Tried to fight
this time, chanted, *No*, writhed
like Delphi's oracle,
then left my body (it's a gift).
After, he performed
an autobiographical rap
for me. I have to laugh
or I'll die.

Hades No. 4: gentle boyfriend,
bug-eyed and mothy
in brown sweaters, reciting facts

about pour-over coffee. Told me
how he fed wine coolers
to his ex, stuck it in her ass
without asking. *That's rape!*
I shouted to our watery
psychiatrist. *I don't think
we can call it that.* Still
took me two months
to dump him. I'm no Persephone.

I Tell My Mother What Happened

In the greenhouse, there are hammers
everywhere. *Pass it to me,* she says,
tacking something for a plant
to grow on. I pluck it from the work
bench, feel all we could
do, together.

My mother was so gentle
when I told her.

Hold this, she is saying. I press
a hand to the lattice

and she pounds the nail in.

I Write Him Notes on My Phone

April 19, 2013, 12:08 AM

I will not be fucking you tonight

Because I'm tired and I have gut rot.
And I'm mad at you for no reason.

April 25, 2013, 1:41 AM

*It was more fun earlier. I hate that
guy. He is a raging homophobe. Plus
he's a raging douche also.*

You do not seem happy at all.

Home? You are basically morose.

I Feel Her Black Temper

He tells me, falls asleep.
It was supposed to be okay.

Times I could roll over, press my lips
between his shoulder blades, kiss along
pointed vertebrae. Boxer shorts
floating over bony hips, cloud-like.

Puppy twitches at our feet. Him,
a puppy, eyelids shivering.

Moon rises over the sill
of his room's small window. My body
drifts inches above the mattress.

Little girl, her face like mine, takes hold
of the ghost of my long hair, leads me to a river
many provinces over where she throws
her body at the water. Willow tips dip
in, storm whips up, she's scooped by a man

who leads her to the place where dead
raspberry canes bump against the white
garage. Trampoline, leaned against the wall
to keep off coming snow.

She grows her black temper.

Awake under bathroom light, faucet
dripping, cold water splitting

my body. What he did to her
pooling at my feet.

Woke up to find me missing. Hear
him breathing in the darkened hall.

Five Spells

after Amber Dawn

1. Forget

Light two candles, one green and one gold. Sea salt
in a bowl, two drops of wintergreen. Incant:
Peace. Still, his body's rough
memory, how his chin dug into your throat, beard
scratches on your inner thighs.

2. Feel the Sun Move from Scorpio to Sagittarius

Begin winter in a new home. Watch your love inject
their gender into thick muscle. Murmur to the ladybug
alighting on your south-facing window, warming her wings
in the now-gentle sun. Soak your bed with queer sex
that makes your body feel like a *fuck you* drum. When the ladybug
dies, bury her carcass in the potted palm.

3. Incant Consent over Your Daughter's Body

Ask before every touch. *May I kiss you? May I wash
you?* Make *no* holy. Untangle the forced compliance
of your own childhood, where you learned your place
as a sacrifice. Make tea with stinging nettle,
raspberry leaf. Your ancestry is thick with witches,
stirring turmeric into milk. *May I kiss you? May I hold you
like this?* Hand her *no* like a blade.

4. Set a Curse

Under the darkest moon, anoint a black candle
with his name. Seal it with an X. When the wax
has burned into a pool, toss it over your shoulder,
never look at it again. You hold the gallows
where they hung your foremothers, your body
an ancestral rope.

5. Give Thanks for the Drink

Take your mother's foul tinctures, brewed with herbs
dug from her own earth with her own hands, ancient
medicine. Drink for the women who say, *I see you,*
who say, *You deserve more.* The ones
who taught you *enough.*

Genealogy

You put violence in me. You breathed
disorder past a tongue ring. My mother
didn't fill up with violence. Her mother

gave up a child before the war and my bones
think that baby came from violence. No history
past mother, aunt, grandmother. Their gentle

hands in my hair. Was my grandmother
filled with violence? Nobody wrote it. Nobody
paid $14.99 to trace their finger up

my mother's Ancestral™ spine. No
Concise Dictionary of Rape. All we have
are bibles. More violence. I say, *My daughter*

won't be filled up with violence. I bash myself
at the walls of my own body. My mother wanted
to protect her sisters, like my grandmother

would have protected my mother, like her mother
and her mother. I say, *I won't let the violence*
touch her, but my palms are glowing, throat

full up with violence, desperate
for my mother's quiet hands.

Artemisia Paints the Violent Deaths of Men

Judith Slaying Holofernes, Artemisia Gentileschi, 1614

Agostino enters the drawing room as the elders
entered the garden, to spy on bathing Susanna. Dueness
bred into men, heinously cultivated, mashed bulldog
snout. He is her tutor, she is eighteen, making masterpieces. 1611,
rape is a crime of damage to property. Found guilty, but Agostino
serves less than a year. She knows how to paint blood. What's changed
since then? Agostino's face for Holofernes, hers for Judith's.
Scholars speculate repressed rage, to which I say, *duh.*

I can't kill you, but in this poem, your life is brutally ended.

Savary

Knees tucked, boulders bracing wind, sunglassed
eyes bird-black. April Sunday, crowds of sand
fleas hopping Mass, my knees the bruisy chapel. Late

morning shuffles over the ridge. Hummingbirds
rumble in Scotch broom, breathless tide keening
to be off. Alone on the beach, pre-tourist, one green

eye reading, one stuck behind its lid. Aware
of feathers spreading, fiddleheads unfolding,
waves forging slices of teal sea glass against

the shore. Later, my pockets full, sneak up
the balcony of an empty mansion, sip
bourbon lemonade and watch red sun melt

the green sea black. Creak the plastic swing set, back
and forth, in and out of heaven. Afterlife, unending
sand fleas whorl, worship the earth into turning.

Down here, tide gasps up the shore on the moon's
leash. I fling sea glass home, an offering. The universe,
the tumbling foxglove. On the beach, legion sand fleas

dance. Heads back, mouths open, drinking sun
from my leg hairs. Reverent of the merest existence,
their small bodies turned towards God.

Galiano 1

Your body ghosts above mine, ass a moon
glow in skylight glass above the loft bed. Stained
tub set into the cabin's floor still filled

with cooling water, where you watched me
wash. *Grey Gardens* on VHS in the background,
Little Edie in her best costume for the day. A week

ago, I shaved my waist-length hair to stubble,
a breakdown. We joke; I'm Edie now. Morning,
you borrow flour from the main house

for pancakes. We walk under January fog,
watch it break over low cliffs, you telling stories
on a spot you used to camp. Never see

another soul, as if the island is ours. I speak
to you in Spanish, gibberish, because you don't
understand but you like the sound. We find

the graveyard, how it's full, no room for more.
This island is done with death. You take photos
that will come out blurry, like botched evidence

of yetis. Hard to prove this weekend ever
happened. The island, grey garden, slowly
masticated by winter moss. In the cold

cabin, we hide from sun. Absorbed
in own little death ritual. Free, for a while,
from the threat of more.

Mayne

Horses listen to the sounds of our 2 AM fighting.
After the car ride, ferry ride, car ride, dog threw up
on the stairs. We forgot to pack

the right kinds of food. Kraft Dinner made with water.
Warm Coke, red wine. My body feels immense, throat
full and aching. Dog's hackles up as I wade

the ditch, feel my way to a warm flank. You are afraid
of horses. I stay up the night, take naked photos
and post them online. I've never felt I was worth more

than my body. Morning, end of us dripping
from spruce branches. Find deer bones on the beach,
spend hours walking the island's length, up and down

under November sun. In the Zen garden, a woman
winds Santa's reindeer in rainbow lights. We fight
evening's push to go inside. Smoke cigarettes

in the hot tub, take off our clothes, try to be
in love. Hot chlorine skin, steaming. Horse
breath rising into the night.

Galiano 2

A woman hangs lights on the wild island; her hands
love them. She is giving fruit to the fruitless: sitka,
douglas, arbutus. Wraps them in plastic vines, bulbed

and glowing white. On a beach nearby, I am flashing
sailors in the bay, throwing up my blouse, my black
dog nosing a fresh fox carcass. Each a kind of love.

Bones creep in with the tide: seal mandible, fish
rib. That night, sailors dream happy dreams. I swim
in bioluminescence, threads of light

in the black waves. How to love like tiny beacons.
Or ritually, like the hanging of lights. Sudden
as goosebumps. My dog is barking at shadows

on shadows. Dogs know how to love. Creatures
who carry creatures who carry light know how
to love. Symbiosis: night birds on black branches, nighthawk

screeching for a mate, finding its lovers
in the dark. A mosquito lands on my wrist; I watch it
drink. Pull a fat tick from my dog's forehead. We're all

so full of love and blood. My flesh rises to meet
a different path. Ahead, my dog barks at glowing night-berries,
winking through the leaves. Night-fruit,

hung so lovingly. All around, like glowing
ocean creatures in the black. Wind chimes rattle
like bones cradled in a blouse. Sailboats creep

over the water. Tomorrow, I will eat gooseberries,
and the dog will bark. I will bury the fox carcass. The woman
will hang more lights, her hands in love.

Spoon

Round of a mixing spoon
against the kitchen wall.
Aches to be full, to scoop
soft things, bear its contents
upward, press to a gentle mouth.

In the wake of my own
flatness; my emptying.

This Job Ends in Six Months
for Jack

You won't remember how we sometimes
sat on the kitchen floor eating berries
from a steel mixing bowl. People won't
smile the way they did on our walks;
matching skin in that city made us mother and son.
Maybe the smell of playground bark,
or the sudden cold of dusk on metal
will make you feel a faraway thing,
but you won't know how I carried you
home through subdivision bones, suburbia
purpling around us. Your breath hot
against my neck, how alone we were. How
I put you in the car, drove circles around
South Dyke Road, your block's strange layers
of city on river on farm. *Mamama*
tumbling from your wet lips, making
me remember that once, I was almost
a mother. I hope in the deep of whoever
you become, there will be the distant,
watery light of us. Tension that left
your body as I held you
against me, as you fell asleep.

Bunny Names

Pregnant, in the field with Aaron,
my favourite student, farm boy.
Our class visits his home. Barn
in back, cattle-dots behind that.
He shows me his bunnies with
bunny names: Hopper, Clover.
Fur soft like Aaron. He touches
the pink of his nose to their noses.
I ask what happens when bunnies
get old. *Eat 'em.* He can eat
what he loves. That night,
I dream of a cow giving birth;
black calf, mother licking caul
from its slick nose, farmer's
shadow face intoning, *Cattle
don't get names.* Blood pooled
at the base of my spine
when I wake. See Aaron's
hair in the wind, and give
my loss a secret name.

All Summer Growing

I had not yet learned
the first lesson of motherhood:
pretend you are brave
until you are brave.

— Rachel Rose, "Notes on Arrival and Departure"

All summer, I'm growing: sugar snaps,
raspberries, fat tomatoes streaked red
and green. Plants are easy to love. My dog
stretched out on the spruce-shade lawn
is easy to love. Flutter in my belly

might be you, might be gas. Too early to tell,
but every night I drip milk. I don't think
I love you yet. You make me barf. Lemon,
bay, spearmint; if you can smell

what I smell, will you love it? Sage, bush
beans, walls of clematis. You're the size
of a mango now. You have genitals. Your guts
are full of tarry black. I must love you,
things you make. What will I make

after you? Tiny lemons dot the tree.
Rhubarb, how it can be poison and dessert
at once. One day, I'll make stepping stones
with your handprints. Your time inside me
like the summer, half-gone.

Eighteen Months

Last daylight in my garden, handful
of eager raspberries, sky burning
pink. Cucumber flowers, taut,
green tomato flesh. The cat noses
at my chin. Mint leaves, lemon balm,
sage, carried in on a basket
of line-dried sheets. Copper kettle,
set to boil. Pause to watch my daughter
sleep. Earlier, her small body
bounded into lake waves, blond
head a bright peony against
the blue. My feeling for her stretches
unpleasantly beyond love.
I can love her
and still feel alone.
Rhubarb leaves hush
against her bedroom window.
My garden this summer,
beginning to bloom.

Universal Miscarriage

I planned to end us, my clutch
of cells. Anyone who's been
a life-giver knows there's no
two 'til long after gestation.
Placed a call, sitting on the kitchen
floor, your eighteen-month-old
would-be sister making dragon
sounds. You were present,
somehow, for bedtime. Little
coyote, rattling my bones
like a howl of boreal breath.
You held me to my guts,
and I thought I could forget
all I really wanted, to see you
slide warm and gooey
from between my legs.
Days after I cancelled,
you fell apart.
Coppery weight
pulsed in my groin
as I watched you swirl
down the shower drain.
Somewhere, your father
crouched over a needle.
Our house crowded
with your quiet death.

Sow Me below Rhubarb

Don't lower my bones down
that eternal elevator. Devour
me for centuries. Not ready
yet, but I'll be a glad ghost,
haunting the corner of your
eye. Not missing you,
reborn as I'll be in the belly
of some distant planet's sun.
If there has to be an epitaph,
let it read: THEY WERE
COMFORTABLE EATING
AT A RESTAURANT ALONE.
Fall to fresh-mud knees,
whorl me in false carnations,
soon to be sun-bleached.
Holler, *He's a bastard, Auntie!*
into my stone's face. I'll
agree. Lastly, let a sunset
be a sunset. Look for me
in your pocket grit.

Mercurial

for John B. McLemore

John B. had church forced on him; hard
to care about who begets whom
in a hot Alabamian chapel. Only child,
no bunk beds in his memory, except
maybe at camp, listening to the hot breath
of the boy above him. Clock-fixer, gilder,
inhaled so much mercury his lungs
were a daguerreotype, spilling chemical breath
and bombastic, accent-thick tirades
on climate change. Other queers
left his heart unroofed; friends said,
If it's such a Shit Town, then leave.
But where is there to go
when the only place that's been kind
is the land your family's buried on?
Flowers, his mother, and his maze
of roses that stippled the earth
in collapsing shadow. Tyler, his foundling,
son and lover, sharpening
blades. John absquatulated Earth,
left him with nothing but stories
of building doors to dank basements, whispers
about buried gold, their initials
spray-painted on a bridge. Impossible
to live when your thoughts are the opposite
of copacetic, and all you can feel
is the pain of re-pierced nipples. Only gold
he owned was made in a cyanide
bucket, coating the inside of this throat.

Revised Survivalist Manifesto

Won't move to northern Idaho, but I might
dig a home from the side of a snowy hill
and quit paying taxes. Do more than one
push-up and chop wood without falling
back into the pile. Cities trouble me,
and I don't buy conspiracies, but
when that mammoth chunk of Antarctic
ice breaks off and lets loose all those
ancient bugs, we're all gonna die
anyway. Charmed as I am by kooks
with their cabals and End-Times,
it's not about guns or Jesus
or the New World Order; this
is misanthropy. Time to get outta Dodge,
keep my kid fearless and poorly
socialized. I'll miss espresso
and antidepressants, but maybe
what Mom's been saying is right:
all I need is a little fresh air.
Learn the difference between
parsnip and hemlock, have dandelion
tea and wild chive salad, cattails
and fiddleheads, rock bass, trout
lily. Before I die, I'll learn
to fall asleep without TV.

Dog Park

Press my face
into piss-soaked earth,
in love with unhappiness.
Dog head cocked, plane
passing slow above. Today
is a day of inertial guilt.
Six hours filling, emptying,
filling my Amazon cart.
Depression and Anxiety:
A Workbook. Someone
fucked up my brain's
plumbing. Incessant
clouds, dog paws
mucky. I won't
have the energy to wipe
them. She was born
in northern Manitoba,
her border collie mother
pushed out four bean-shaped
sacs, highway-side.
She's nosing me;
get up soon or someone
will see us,
and my weirdness
will be too much.
If it was as simple
as rain, or pills,
I would have solved it
by now. Flick grass
from my face.
The dog is happy.

Pat & Vanna

He'd known her for five years
when her fiancé's plane went
down over Van Nuys. One
week of the wheel's *tick tick*
tick tick and she was back,
teeth gleaming, slinky in '86
backless shimmer. Announced
her first pregnancy in '92
with a puzzle, solved: VANNA'S
PREGNANT, her tap gentle
on the lights, his eyes wet. She
miscarried before the episode
aired, producers thank god-ing.
He laid a hand on hers under
hot dressing room lights. Never
like that with them; son of Polish
immigrants and her, half Puerto
Rican, last name of her stepfather
crisp on the announcer's lips.
Together longer than spouses,
than some siblings, still stepping
out each night under carnival
lights, filming promos in Hawaii,
smirking at how awkward Trebek
can be after all this time. Mai tais
late at the hotel bar, no need
to speak of their strange fate,
dealt from the major arcana.
Cicadas clicking in the night, like
their wheel that spins the world.

The Women Hikers of Halfmoon Bay

Four of them, rising early, elbow-deep
in rubber gloves, take to ditches, their 5 K
of Highway 101. They exist. They have
a blue billboard. Pulp trucks honk. From
the road, you can't see green water, mountains
low-slung, Galapagosian beauty of their other-
world. How they met grey hair scarcely
remembers, or whose damn idea this was
anyway. A lot hangs unspoken in the 6 AM
air. *Nana* and *Auntie* and *Mom* are words
like *spoon;* say them enough and they lose
all meaning. Four mothers stabbing trash.
Four wives, husbands retired, rounded on
artisan potato chips. Someone had a party
with vibrators for sale, blond woman in a lab
coat spouting *sexual peak!* They've come
to prefer trails, comfort of unexplained
understandings, not needing to shave. After all,
there's no sex at the end. No husbands. Death
is all over the highway; animal bones, used
condoms. Every car that passes is death. Every
plastic bag will outlive them by a million years.
At death, there will be women. Nobody is born
in a room full of men. Four women picking garbage,
quiet. Sun and moon together in the sky.

One of Many Ways to Be a Bad Mother

Obituary says he lived to serve the Lord. Seven years old, one of many
little lambs. Day his mother took a bath,
he revved the four-wheeler, whirled around the back
forty. Too far to hear. Cool bathwater, so hot outside cattle
rippled and warped, low buzz of summer and the smell
of heat in the cedar trees. He tangled
in razor wire. She told them all a thousand times.

Too far to hear his slow rip from the earth. She leaned back
and shut her eyes, stretched her pruney toes. Sighed.

A Girl Like This Might Have Loved Glenn Gould

We meet under the four-tonne goose. April, I wear a parka, slush
underfoot. He's humming, tongue knocking Bach against
hard palate; I feel it knock against me. *They only just
built it*, I tell him, it's 1966, my seventeen knocks against his
thirty-four. *Why do they call you Wawa*, he asks, as if
I *am* the town. I eye the statue, *It means*

goose. He eats breakfast at the Kinniwabi Pines, sometimes
brings his typewriter, wipes the rim of his mug pre-sip. I waitress,
bring infinite eggs, read over his shoulder, *The Idea of North*. Men
from MacLeod Mine call him funny for not shaking hands, fur hat
in the middle of May. My father, no wife to shush him, hurls
Yer a nutter! from the corner booth, diagnosis

unnoticed by the pianist at the counter. June and still wearing
his wool coat indoors, kids outside in shorts, throwing
old snow around. I hear he has a place on Superior, disappears
nightly over that cold ocean. Disappears, I hear, up Highway 17,
Top 40 on the radio, someone tells him Wawa isn't nothing
of North; his Toronto is showing. Hides it across Superior's

forehead: Nipigon, Red Rock, Thunder Bay to Kenora, reels of tape
holding voices who came to be or were born into it, this Northern
life. I graduate; wait through July to hear him on the CBC, that small
body thrusting into piano, eyes shut or else locked
on the work of hurried fingers. In the bath, I learn to look at my own
body, its possibilities. Soft underwater, butt-end

cozied to the removable shower head. Too poor for a piano but my father
and I listen to the Met on Saturday mornings. August,
the pianist is back, scrambled eggs and fingers scrambling

over typewriter keys. I worry he can smell me when I sweat through
my uniform, find myself trying to find him outside, sometimes
near the port in Michipicoten or Queens Park under

the goose. This Queen's park against Toronto's, caroming
behind his eyes, fingers bouncing Goldberg Variations on his thigh; to be under
those fingers. September, some of my friends
move to Toronto but I'm here, pianist at the counter, running
a fever. My father in the corner booth, displeasure
blooming like wild irises as he watches me lay a cool palm on the pianist's

forehead, my palm the weather here. He leans in, asks to interview
me, *We could meet under the goose, okay?* After work, I'm smeared with lipstick
that was my mother's, eighty degrees under that goose
and he has long sleeves on. Clicks the tape recorder, *Do you like*
Bob Dylan? You're a real-live Girl from the North Country. Tell him about pike
fishing, my father, the mine. *My mother was a white-passing*

Métis woman. She died when I was born. He asks, *Will you ever leave*
this place? Maybe, I say, knowing I won't. After, he gives me a ride,
windows down, Streisand rattling out of the old radio. Home, wild
irises from my father in a vase. Next day, pianist at the counter, his usual,
no more words than that for me. October, cold air sniffing
at my ankles, and he's gone. Back East, I hear, to finish

his work. I wander in the shortening days, whistle Little Fugue. Weeks
later, my father and I listening to the CBC, *my baby's famous.* Wait to hear
my voice and when it never comes, pat on the shoulder and left
alone. As if none of it happened. I shut my eyes, think of coming
snow. Gentle snoring from my father's room. November, all the leaves
nearly fallen, frost on grass in the morning.

Picnic Bench, Permanent Marker

In the 1700 Rainy River shore was at fire no 127 Bone Road
Along side driveway and side of house backyard area
Man from Montreal had trouble with his sail and
broke his dark lens. A lot of water, yes

i.

Nowadays, there's a bend in the river one klick
from fire number 127 Bone Road. Around 2005, his dad
drops him off five klicks from there to walk home. To teach
a lesson. On the way he passes the corner where his best
friend will die in a car wreck two years later. In the 1700s,
there was no Bone road, no fire number 127, but the river
hiked up its shore anyhow and tiptoed, bowlegged,
to meet something.

ii.

The earth alongside driveway (side of house, backyard area)
holds onto virtues of a riverbed for three hundred years. Houses rise
and fall and rise again. River grass wobbles behind a 1990s
rancher. People move in, have babies. His father falls
from a roof onto thick river muck and starts gobbling
pain pills. Water lilies drift into the air on frail roots;
cattails thump their brown heads together.

iii.

The man from Ville-Marie, *vexé contre la voile*. It's ripped
or it won't lift; the river and the boat conspired
to wash him up on someone's back step, *désolé de vous déranger*.
Broken shards of dark glass. Three hundred years later, some *lignée*
had a story for a picnic bench; a man, maybe, who forgot his pills.

iv.

The champ of size 13 Converse low-tops on gravel. Sounds
a lot like the ruin of a pair of polarized three-hundred-dollar Oakleys
against the hull of an aluminum fishing boat. He's heading
for the address the river kissed. TV-lit room, his father sleeping
in the La-Z-Boy. Son, filled with what he doesn't know.
His body overflowing, as with a lot of water, yes.

Eighteen Anamneses

for Lizzie Borden

I. Things belly their way in, furred, many-legged; she cups them
   to her.

II. They are kept in almost-large alcove; she, her little sister, never
   leaving. Many bits of old paper around.

III. Not Fall River (1892). She is not *that* Lizzie and also
   she is. She knows about hatchets.

IV. Here is a scrap: R-A-T, B-A-T, C-A-T; learn to spell them,
   there they are, vocabulary-creatures.

V. She is moon-eyed and wild and rarely eats breakfast. She is
   fifteen and thirty at once.

VI. A flock of pigeons gets in and roosts on her so she
   is made of birds.

VII. Rats scoot across rooftops; attic-bound, up high
   they can watch. Wish to be rats.

VIII. Roosting pigeons, pets, put to hatchet-death by the father
   who keeps them (girls, not pigeons).

IX. Another scrap: *I am a witch! Pentagram, pentagram, pentagram! What
   is a pentagram? What? WHAT?!* (poem)

X. Girls, kept penned and comfortable with all sorts of a man's
   malevolence.

XI. If only to be Hecate. Hatchets, though, are heavy
   with their own memories.

XII. Lizzie squiggles down while a man is sleeping. To the hatchet,
her power blooms up the handle.

XIII. A man's eyeball split in half, mulch-coloured iris. Skull
whacked, sneakily.

XIV. A call placed to 911, screaming *Help!* lyrics. (joke)

XV. Gross, what a body can do to another when all a body has
is itself, its memories.

XVI. Little sister helps Lizzie burn her clothes. And his clothes. They keep
the hatchet.

XVII. No one thinks to wonder if the sisters had done
it. They fix up the place, keep pets.

XVIII. Last scrap: *I am a horror. It's wonderful to be a horror and to live
in a house that's mine.*

Two Virgos

Hermits of the Tarot, I daydream about reading
your cards somewhere on a rainy afternoon.
Remember when I kissed you after Pride
then passed out drunk? Now, we're two provinces
apart. You don't want children; I already have
one. You sent valerian tea for my birthday;
I sent flowers for yours, wafts of peony, bluebells.
The tea was meant to soothe me. Or maybe
you just had it lying around, like my aunt who
keeps a closet of gifts for no one in particular.
Valerian calms, but my cheeks are flushed,
heart beating hummingbird-quick. I believe
there's a universe where we knit together
on the couch, toes barely touching. Quietly
sipping from twin mugs of heat.

Hashime Murayama with My Legs Stirrup-Splayed

Hashime watercoloured gladiola, sunfish,
cells swept from pursed lips of cervices,
smeared across laboratory glass. Paint
blotting into tight drops of normal nuclei
next to frantic duplicity of squamous
carcinoma, those slumping blobs hunched
on the slide, two-eyed, frightened
as newborn ghosts. Hashime's eye
to the microscope, finding no romance
in Pap smear's cancer, how it streamed
magenta through cytoplasmic rivers of cyan,
multiplying infinitely, antiseptic-scented
rooms echoing catch-in-throat news.
Seventy years later I wait for swab's
keen pressure, bum-up with legs stirrup-
splayed. Hashime's name snug in the corner
of *Painting of Several Spiders at Work*
on the office wall, their spindle-limbs
shrouding cicadas in silk. Shut my eyes
against fluorescence, see Hashime work
backwards, painting cells into petals
and scales, brushing my own sharp streak
of magenta back into flowers and fish.

Tree Planters

On their cellphones at Safeway,
the public library. Brown legs,
undercuts. I forget I've five years
on them; they still wear headbands
and Nirvana T-shirts, legs
unshaven, armpits loamy. A kid,
they made my legs tremble. Took boys
and girls to bed, rubbed up
against a decorative
pillow. Now, they eye
my tattoos in the canned-goods
aisle. I could always
offer to buy someone's jar
of olives. No worries
for the baby scar on my belly.
They're only in town
for the night.

Bright, Heavy Things
for Alex

I'm three to your four when your small
head slumps onto my shoulder
in the cancer clinic waiting room. Around us,
bald children play, sad-eyed mothers watching.

You scream when they pull out the wires
that took poison to your heart. I ask
for more candy from the wood-panelled
machine. Your bedside table, covered
with offerings: seashells from the farmer's
market, Happy Meal toys. A fist-sized
chunk of amethyst dug, mysteriously,
from under the neighbour's fence.

I run my finger over skin-graft bumps
on your thigh while you squirm; no one
must ask to touch you.

At Ronald McDonald House, sick kids
watch their siblings play foosball. Moms
crowd in the kitchen, too weary to fight
Popsicles for dinner.

When it's over, we go back to our game
of seeing who can toss Barbie higher
into the tall blue spruce. Cancer ate one year.
My memory stretches it to many;
in yours, it's stretched so thin it disappears.

Years later, they find a knot of tumour
nestled in the thickness of your bicep.
I want to chew it like a rotten cherry,
spit its pit between my teeth into the wind.

Audrey's House

Her windows and bathroom
walls were crusty
with adhesive
from decorative window
hangings. Audrey, we learned
from the neighbours; house
sold to us by her son,
his initials,
P.R., appearing over
and over under every
layer of wood panelling
and old carpet
we peeled away.
Her garden, three years
without her, reduced
to strange mounds,
bursts of iris and a half-
dead apple tree.
Our first nights,
I burned sage, promised
spring in this place
where she spent
seventy years. Kept
her prescriptions
stuck to the inside
of kitchen cabinets, red
label-maker message:
THINK TALL YOU MIGHT GROW.
Planted spearmint
and thyme, hyssop,
peony, yellow dahlias
below the window, ripped

grass from around
the climbing rose,
exhumed daylily bulbs,
gnarls of tuber packed
tight as a sac of glands,
harvestmen resting
on my wrists.
Generations of insects
displaced as I pried shards
of cement from the earth,
like pieces of a grave,
soft clicking of spruce
beetles in my ears
as I pushed through
a thin film of her
composted hair,
like pushing tenderly
through her skull.
She sits with us
at night, while
we watch TV
in her living room,
houseplants rusting
against her breath.

Girls Who

Tucked arms inside parkas, winter recess,
tied each other's sleeves tight
over chests. Knot at the heart, way
of keeping warm. Girls who said,
We're playing alone, which meant
together, but not with you. The girls
who sang "American Pie" in the spring
talent show and "Silent Night"
at the Christmas pageant. Who wept
when you were picked to play
Mary, so you gave it up,
played a sheep. Every birthday,
skinny-dipped at Sand Point,
how you tracked the progress
of each other's bodies,
shiny under moonlight.
The girls who roasted weenies
and filled their bathing suits with sand
to look like boobs, who gave you CDs
and drank Coke and didn't speak
to you on Monday. Girls
who cut off your bangs
while you slept, who played Spice Girls
and made you be Sporty.
Got infections in their belly rings,
got high at parties, got asked
to dance during Snowball. Kissed you
in the basement, lights flashing green
and blue, lips stained pink and sweet
with Sour Puss. The girls who were endlessly
spinning, whose boyfriends died

in car crashes, whose bodies
became sacrifice. The girls
who passed tampons under
bathroom stall doors.

Board

for Drew

im going to throw myself off a bridge im so board

Two-by-four, maple or ash, hucked
at hard snow behind his parents' house. Melted,
now frozen again. Board's corners skitter
over whited-out lawn.

too bad there aren't any bridges there

i'll build one

No river either, back in the yard, no
deep. Nothing to wrap a bridge
around. His would straddle an empty
field, gather snow onto its back.

then you'll have something to do, and you won't need it

it'll be a boring bridge

Or a lonely one. Confused
at how it came to stand there, with nothing
but the stars between its knees.

Ritual Loop

We are hot inside; we are afraid
outside. Myself and my disorder
self. Chest and throat being full
of something. Pressing against.
Plein: word tries to skitter, no
space for playful. Let's take a photo
of ourself with room, blue cup
and jasmine. A person, a flower.
One tilts its chin, tilt (1) tilt (2)
tilt (3) tilt (4), one cranes its many
necks toward the window. We should
leave. Things here need adjustment.
Let's touch them. Empty our throat
of the something. We feel bad about
nice weather. Let's tap the computer
with our nail twenty times. Do that four times
more. Let's smack ourself, four times
on the forehead. Repeat it, rightly.

Loop. Remember
what it meant in years before disorder:
white wool dyed with Kool-Aid,
sunned and neon, circling our fingers,
needles, making something to be worn.
Days repeating and repeating. *Rempli.*
Now, only us, and the something.
Tearing petals to quiet its drum.

Dad's Not Good on the Phone

Shoulder creaks as he pulls against his limp, knee
a couple months old, titanium hip. Buzzing,
his hands rustle, few seconds then he passes
the receiver, *Here's your mother.* Emails later:

> *How big of a bird bath will it take to let me flap.*
> *Sore left wing and when I rest it I go around in circles.*
> *A lot better now but it still drags in the water.*

He makes me wonder who the poet is. Inherited his love
of maps, lakes, lines that point. Planning
our goat farm, our boat ride down the Mississippi,
how in his mind he might live forever.

The two of us, restless, pulling against
ourselves, fighting about fractions, parallel parking,
or why he never taught me to sail.

> *I brought the glider rocker in from the boat so we can all see the TV.*
> *That was Mom's idea.*

She is at the centre of our tempers, our flapping
need, cleaning our smears of bright paint. Refilling feeders,
stone basins, unaware of her own loveliness. Ear out
for the trill of the telephone.

Morning in her garden, while he gets stoned
on his boat, landlocked
behind the garage.

Clearwater

You pass me the fish's heart.
Outside the gut-hut, clouds
pile on clouds. We are shadows
on the clear lake, long wooden
table slick with viscera, hole over gut
bucket, *schlick* of knife on flesh.
Woman with bright lips, her tiny
trout gleaming coral and green.
Hook she pulls from its chest
an answer. Her eyeshadow
flashes like scales. You hold
a translucent filet in each brown
hand. We are fifteen; the lake
is ageless. Its belly put out the sun.
All this time, the fish's heart
beating. Gasping for blood
in the dip of my palm.

Reading Sharon Olds in the Tub

Pick the golden Pulitzer Prize sticker
from the cover of *Stag's Leap*, slap it
on a bottle of conditioner. My jaw's insectile
clicking echoes off the mouldy tile. When
she finds the mistress's picture in her husband's
trouser pocket, I think of shaking dirty work
jeans, hydromorph shells skittering under
the dryer. Sharon's lack of bitterness freaks
me out; mine's an oily glaze on the surface
of the water. My husband cheated on me
with heroin, but I was never really honest,
and I'm lovingly green at Sharon's
high ground. I stroke the stag's
furred belly, moored by a person who will
never know me; this is poetry. Stick
my ears under, crack the spine, start again.

Wedding

Oregon in February, grey with pathetic fallacy.
The fact that you couldn't look at the black ocean
at night isn't for the sake of metaphor; you really
couldn't look. It reminded you of the distance
within yourself. At the top of the switchback road,
wind was forcing whale-sized waves up the cliffside,
as you cupped your cigarette between appropriately
ragged hands. Bride and groom stumbled from the forest,
trailed by a damp photographer, his umbrella inside-out.
Gust snatched the bride's veil, five of us watching
dizzily as it disappeared into the flat, white sky.

Husband

after Ken Babstock

Fourteen, fingers slippery with each other.
Wet trampoline, his Baptist mother. *The Wall*
in his basement. Bologna. Bareback. Baby robin
falls on the grass. Grow up to haunt the same city;
he's an East Van sack-o-bones, I shave my head
to feel pretty. In Chinatown, he tells his story:
I quit. Drops his skateboard down the cement steps,
splits. Pushing thirty, we fuck under the blood moon,
crescent of pinholes tucked under his wrist. Soon,
I will shuck this body. Drift into the courthouse
on pink tulle scales as I devour my tail.

Compulsory

When I was little, I got off in itchy
church tights. Rubbed against *LOVE*
embroidered on a pillow, thinking
about breasts from my dad's form
drawing books. When I was a child,
I played mortician with a girl I loved;
we said her red socks were blood.
She put pretend makeup on my dead
girl face, my brain tingling. I grew
up a bit, got boys off. So many boys,
their little dicks. Hand jobs, blow jobs,
love currency. Brought home boyfriend
after boyfriend, but I still thought about
girls, kissed girls in front of boys. Girls
didn't count. When I grew all the way
up, I fucked boys, thinking, *If I was gay,*
I'd have done it by now. Loved a girl
who stood in the kitchen, peeling
oranges. Pounded boys into my own
head, checking boxes, waiting for a click.
I married a boy to cure myself of love,
spellbound by the world's approval,
red socks tucked in back of my mind.

Not Puddles

Not queer enough, too stealth. Not
straight at-fucking-all.
Not the white-gay-men-next-door.
Not men, not women. Not *the guy*
with your face, fuzzy. Not *the girl* with my skirt,
tight. Not solid at the knees
after you fuck me into a puddle.
Your puddle, it's bigger than mine. Not
presenting our bepuddled sheets
to The Committee of Confused
but Well-Intentioned Straight People,
for them to divine, based on puddle-
density/size, once and for all,
who really is the fucking Guy.™
Or to the Grand High Council
of Gay Witches, who measure
our dildos, You must be THIS LONG
to enter the gay bar
without being side-eyed. Not
giving the drunk fuckhead
at the party a roadmap
of our junk. Not explaining why
I wouldn't rather fuck a *real* guy
with a Disappointment Guaranteed
bloodflow dick. Why I'd rather
fucking die. Not letting you get beat
up in the bathroom. I have bear
mace in my bag.

Quitting My Meds

My eyes burn into the soup.
On the windowsill, square pills,
halved. Three years, levelled
by their pale pink chemicals.
We want to have a baby.
Your egg, my womb, donor
unknown. You'll have to quit,
too. Testosterone blocks
your shedding. Say
you'll hibernate if the fur
drops from your face
and your waist reappears,
death-rumble of your before-ness.
I remember I used to get
angry. Didn't know how
to stop sleeping with men,
deriving their traumas,
squeezing ice cubes 'til
my hands were numb
to distract myself from death,
playing *one hand in the grave.*
Hours, now, since I took
just half. Crying
onion tears. Waiting
for the soup to boil.

Kandinsky

after Cara Kauhane

When you tell me you want
to die, blocks of colour
erupt behind my shut eyes.
Mouldable and yielding,
like kindergarten Plasticine;
textured, some striped,
lumpy, blast their blue
and purple/red bodies
across my brain, Kandinsky's
circles gone telescopic. *Schlook!*
Tragic synesthesia.
Yellow gun vomiting supple,
bimorphic forms. I press
my forehead, you want me
to say something.

Lean quietly my colour-
spinning body
into yours.

January 5

> I write about you all the time, I said aloud.
> Every time I say "I," it refers to you.
>
> — Louise Glück, "Visitors from Abroad"

2017

In my dream, your face
splits with hurt,
screaming my old promise
that I would never
feel better.

I'm confused, then
I understand; you are twenty,
and deserve to behave
like any other twenty-year-old,
like I did.

I don't feel better, I say.

2016

Every year for thirteen years
my mother and I
bring you an ice candle
on Christmas Eve.

Remember the year
your brother was there,
shovelling furiously,
unburying you.

On the fourteenth year,
we stop.

2015

Your birthday and my daughter's,
two days apart. Odd,
to be seven years older
than you will ever be,
when you were always
the one who was
seven years older.

She is born
in a snowstorm,
and has your name.

2013

I tell our aunt
how your death
was *especially hard*
on me.

It was hard on all of us,
she says, kindly. I'd held on
to my teenager's belief
in superlative pain.

She gives me your blue
Swiss Army knife,
and I wear it on a chain
around my neck.

2010

I ask my therapist
why I don't dream
about you. *Maybe*
you do, she says.
I like to think
there is a dream world
where we are happy.

Therapist says,
Try to see yourself
as she saw you.

A way to cure
my self-loathing.
It doesn't work.

Instead, I write
bad poems about you,
and the ridiculous
hole in my heart
gets me into
a writing program.

2003

After, my mother and yours,
your sister, aunts,
our girl cousins,
spread your diaries
on pale blue
living room carpet,
your autopsy.

I never knew
you wrote poems.

2017

When I wake up, the dream
is on my chest, looking at me.

We make an ice candle
for your birthday,
leave it burning on the steps
through the night.

Notes

"A Girl Like This Might Have Loved Glenn Gould" won the *Malahat Review's* Open Season Award for Poetry in 2014. "This Job Ends in Six Months" appeared in *Best Canadian Poetry in English* (Tightrope Books, 2016). "Galiano 2" appeared in *30/30* (In/Words Press, 2017). "Mercurial" received third place in *CV2's* 2-Day Poem Contest in 2017.

The two parts of "I Write Him Notes on My Phone" are unedited, taken from the Notes app on my iPhone.

The italicized text that makes up the first part of "Picnic Bench/Permanent Marker" is a fragment I found written with Sharpie on a picnic bench at Seven Oaks Park in Fort Frances, Ontario, in May of 2013.

Acknowledgements

Poems from this book have appeared previously, sometimes slightly altered, in the *Malahat Review, ARC Poetry Magazine*, the *Dalhousie Review, Plenitude Magazine*, the *Puritan*, the *New Quarterly*, the *Fiddlehead, QWERTY, EVENT Magazine, SAD Magazine*, and *CV2*. Thank you to the editors of each magazine.

Thank you to my parents, Bob and Cis Barron, for your support, generosity, and deep love.

Thank you to Rhea Tregebov for mentorship and friendship. Thank you also to Nancy Lee for your notes on an earlier version of this manuscript.

Thank you to my wonderful peers and workshop pals for your time and insight, as well as your friendship. Thank you, especially, to Ellie Sawatzky for treating my poems with so much thoughtful tenderness.

Thank you to Reece Cochrane for friendship, support, and some lovely background music.

Thank you to Leah Horlick for your thoughtful editing and for providing so much inspiration through your own brilliant work.

To everyone at Goose Lane Editions/icehouse poetry: thank you for believing in this book and for your hard work in making it a reality.

Thank you to all survivors, for your bravery in telling your stories, and for believing and honouring mine.

Thank you to Anouk and Wynne, my little family. You make life possible.

Joelle Barron is a writer living as a settler on the traditional territory of the Anishinaabe of Treaty 3 (Kenora, ON). They received an MFA in Creative Writing from the University of British Columbia in 2014. Their poems have appeared in several magazines, including *ARC Poetry Magazine*, *Plenitude Magazine*, the *New Quarterly*, and *SAD Mag*. "A Girl Like This Might Have Loved Glenn Gould" won the *Malahat Review*'s Open Season Award in 2014; "Mercurial" placed third in *CV2*'s 2-Day Poem Contest in 2017. Joelle works as a co-ordinator for SPACE, an LGBT2S+ youth group.